VERSAILLES

STROLLING THROUGH
THE ROYAL ESTATE

Photography: Jacques GIRARD
René-Paul PAYEN, Jean-Claude VARGA
Plans: Pierre BEQUET, Michel LEFEBVRE
Design: Jacques GIRARD
Assistant Designer: Pierre KEGELS
Copyright : Editions d'Art Lys

Typesetting and Photo-engraving
BUSSIERE ARTS GRAPHIQUES - Paris
Third edition in French
by T.M.R.
In Fontenay-sous-Bois
Copyright 2nd trimestre 1983

GERALD VAN DER KEMP
Membre de l'Institut
Inspecteur Général Honoraire des Musées

DANIEL MEYER
Conservateur au Musée National
des Châteaux de Versailles et de Trianon

VERSAILLES

STROLLING THROUGH
THE ROYAL ESTATE

Translation : Bronia Fuchs

ÉDITIONS D'ART LYS

CONTENTS

INTRODUCTION 5
PLAN OF ENTRANCES TO THE ROYAL ESTATE 7
SEVERAL DATES 8
GENERAL PLAN OF THE CHATEAU 10

THE CHATEAU 12

THE ENTRANCE COURTYARDS 12
THE 17th CENTURY ROOMS 14
THE ROYAL CHAPEL 17
THE HERCULES ROOM 18
PLAN OF THE FIRST FLOOR OF THE CHATEAU 20
THE STATE APARTMENT 22
THE HALL OF MIRRORS 32
THE QUEEN'S APARTMENT 35
THE CORONATION ROOM AND 1792 ROOM 43
THE HALL OF BATTLES 45
THE QUEEN'S STAIRCASE 47
THE KING'S APARTMENT 48
THE KING'S PRIVATE SUITE 54
Mme DE MAINTENON'S APARTMENT 64
THE QUEEN'S PRIVATE CABINETS 65
THE KING'S PRIVATE APARTMENTS 68
THE ROYAL OPERA 70
THE 18th CENTURY ROOMS 72
THE CONSULATE AND EMPIRE ROOMS 74
THE 19th CENTURY ROOMS 75

THE GARDENS 77

PLAN OF THE GARDENS 78
THE EAST-WEST AXIS 80
THE NORTH-SOUTH AXIS 92
THE GROVES 103

TRIANON 107

THE GRAND TRIANON 107
TOUR OF THE GRAND TRIANON 108
THE SMALL TRIANON 118
PLAN OF MARIE-ANTOINETTE'S HAMLET 124
GENEALOGY 128

INTRODUCTION

This small guide to Versailles and Trianon is not intended as an exhaustive study of the most famous château in the world. A large number of works and erudite articles on the subject already exist and much still remains to be said concerning details not only of the architecture of the château but also of its interior decoration and the gardens. However, this has by no means been our aim in this booklet.

Our intention here is to offer an easily accessible work to guide the tourist in his visit to Versailles. It is for this reason that is seemed to us more important to discuss in greater détail the apartments which may be visited freely than those of which guided tours are organized. As the Museum of French History is at present being reorganized, we have simply given some general information on this museum.

We did not wish, either, to give a detailed history of the château's construction. A chronological table seemed to us to be far more useful and clear to the visitor to Versailles. This introduction will simply bring out the uniqueness of this palace.

Louis XIII, the son of Henri IV, was born at Fontainebleau on 14th September 1601. During his reign, royal authority was strengthened with the help of the chief minister, Richelieu. He died at Saint-Germain-en-Laye on 14th May 1643.

Originally a small hunting pavilion erected in 1624 by Louis XIII who had it rebuilt in 1631, Versailles very soon attracted Louis XIV. The Sun King had construction work carried out on an increasingly large scale between 1661 and 1681. On 6th May 1682, he decided to make it the Court residence and seat of Government, which Versailles remained until 6th October 1789 when the royal family was forced by the Revolution to return to Paris and take up residence in the Tuileries.

Versailles was, therefore, the capital of France for more than one hundred years; it was a veritable administrative city, with ministries and lodgings for the Court officials. In fact, only the central section served as the King's residence. The south and north wings (with the Chapel and Opera attached to the latter) were reserved for the Princes and people holding office at Court.

On either side of the Great Courtyard, the Ministers' Wings were the administrative centre; behind the southern Ministers' Wing were the lodgings for the King's personal staff. The King's Stables and coachhouses stood opposite the château, beyond the Royal Parade Ground. Other buildings were erected gradually as the need arose : the Directors' and Chancellor's Offices, the Queen's Stables.

Louis XIII's son, Louis XIV, was born at Saint-Germain-en-Laye on 5th September 1638. After his personal reign which marked the pinnacle of the French monarchy's glory, he died at Versailles on 1st September 1715.

Louis XV, great grandson of Louis XIV, was born at Versailles on 15th February 1710. During his reign, French civilization spread throughout Europe. He died at Versailles on 10th May 1774.

Under Louis XV, the Ministeries of War and Foreign Affairs, which had been given insufficient room in the Ministers' Wings, were installed in new buildings south of the Great Outhouses. One can therefore say that "the whole of French history" took place at Versailles during the reigns of Louis XIV, Louis XV and Louis XVI. However, it was also at Versailles that one of the most privileged moments in the flowering of art in all its forms occurred : before the Revolution, the château was a veritable museum where everyone was admitted "if he was decently dressed". The collections in the Louvre Museum, the Bibliothèque Nationale (National Library), the Jardin des Plantes and the Cabinet of Medallions were built up from those of the various sovereigns who were also great lovers of music, literature and the theatre and made their capital the European centre of 17th and 18th civilization.

Stripped of its masterpieces during the Revolution and restored by Napoleon and Louis XVIII (who were never able to live there), it seemed that Versailles would have to be abandoned and perhaps destroyed, when Louis-Philippe decided to transform it into a "Museum dedicated to all the Glories of France", using his personal finances. It was the task of our century to continue the reorganization of the museum begun by Pierre de Nolhac and, after paring down the collections, to decide how the works were

Louis XVI was born at Versailles on 25th August 1754. He was unable to repress the inevitable outbreak of the Revolution and died on the scaffold on 21st January 1793.

to be grouped : for example, the 17th century works were to be placed in the north wing against a background of fabrics woven from original designs; the 18th century paintings were hung on the ground-floor of the central section, in rooms whose pre-Revolution décor is gradually being restored, and the attic storeys were chosen for works of the Consulate and Empire periods — they were placed against fabrics which recall the imperial palaces. However, the main attraction for visitors to Versailles is the former residence of the Kings of France. While the "royal beauty" which once aroused the wonder of Louis XIV's contemporaries cannot be revived, the efforts undertaken over the last thirty years have recreated the décors known by Louis XV and Louis XVI.

The first spectacular work of restoration was that of the Opera, followed by the King's Private Cabinet and his Games Room, the Room of the Queen's Gentlemen and her Bedchamber and, finally, the Hall of Mirrors and Louis XIV's Bedchamber.

At the same time, the mark left on the Grand Trianon by Napoleon has been given renewed splendour and the elegance bestowed on the Small Trianon by Marie-Antoinette has been recreated there.

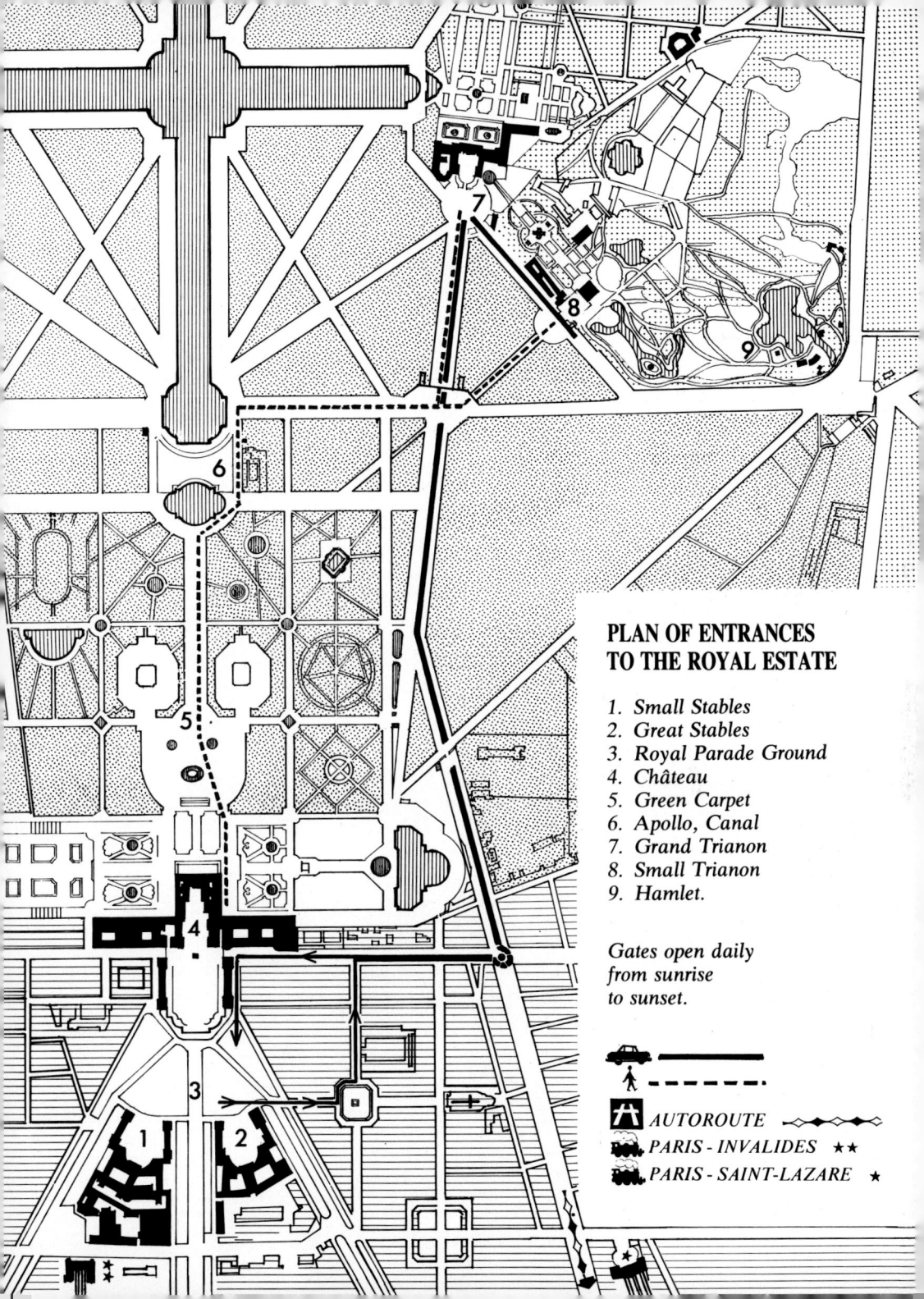

1624 Louis XIII's first hunting château.
1631 Second château, built by Philibert Le Roy.
1661 Louis XIV's first investment in Versailles.
1662 Château renovated and gardens embellished.
1663 First Orangery and Menagerie by Le Vau.
1664 Festivities called "The Pleasures of the Enchanted Island".
1665 First statues placed in the gardens. Grotto of Tethys.
1667 The Grand Canal.
1668 Construction of Le Vau's "envelope" on the gardens side. The Great Royal Entertainment.
1670 The Porcelain Trianon.
1671 Le Brun begins the decoration of the State Apartments.
1672 The Bathing Apartment.
1674 Great Commission of 24 statues designed by Le Brun. Last of the three great celebrations held by Louis XIV.
1678 Hall of Mirrors (completed in 1686). Ambassadors' Staircase. South Wing (completed in 1682).
1682 Versailles becomes the seat of Government.
1684 The Orangery (completed in 1686).
1685 North Wing, (completed in 1689).
1687 Marble Trianon.
1710 Consecration of the new Chapel.
1738 Beginning of large-scale work on the Private Cabinets.
1750 French Pavilion.
1762 Small Trianon, (completed in 1768).
1770 Inauguration of the Opera.
1771 Construction of the "Gabriel Wing".
1783 Queen's Hamlet in the Small Trianon.
1789 The King leaves Versailles.
1792 The Convention decides on the sale of the royal furniture.
1837 Louis-Philippe inaugurates the Museum of French History.
1952 Restoration of the Opera, (completed in 1957).
1962 Restoration of the Grand Trianon, (completed in 1966).
1975 Reconstruction of the Queen's Bedchamber.
1980 Restoration of Louis XIV's Bedchamber and the Hall of Mirrors.

Versailles, circa 1668, by Pierre Patel

ATTIC STOREY

A. Ceiling of the Hall of Mirrors
B. Chimay Attic Directory and Consulate Rooms*
C. Coronation Room Ceiling
D. South Attic Empire Rooms*
E. Ceiling of the Hall of Battles
F. Mme de Pompadour's Apartment
G. Mme du Barry's Apartment*
H. The King's Private Apartments*

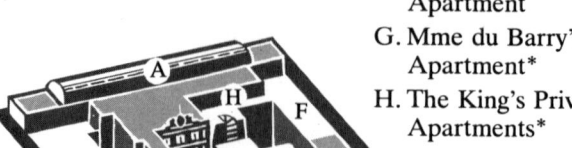
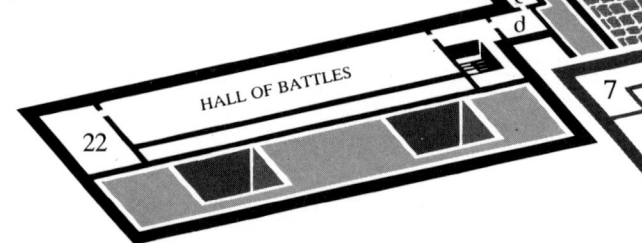

FOR
THE FIRST FLOOR
SEE
DETAILED PLAN
PAGE 20

GROUND-FLOOR

1. Lower Chapel Vestibule
2. 17th Century Rooms
3. Crusade Rooms
4. Madame Victoire's Apartment
5. Madame Adélaïde's Apartment
6. Marie-Antoinette's Apartment
7. The Dauphin's Apartment
8. The Dauphine's Apartment
9. The Princes' Staircase
10. Rooms of the Napoleonic Epos

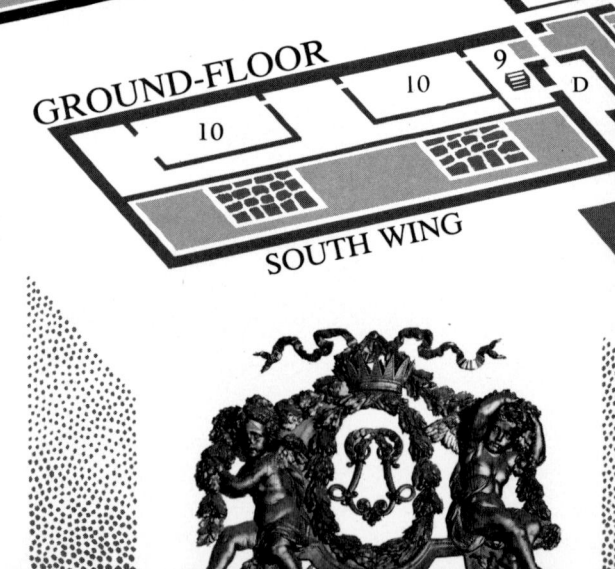

*The château is open from 9.45 a.m. to 5. p.m.
Closed on Mondays and holidays.
* Conducted tours are available by
National Museum guides.
For information concerning admission charges
and regular tour schedules,
or to request special tours,
please ring the château of Versailles,
950.58.32*

FIRST FLOOR

11. 17th Century Rooms
12. 19th Century Rooms
13. Upper Chapel Vestibule
14. Hercules Room
15. State Apartment
16. The King's Private Suite
17. The King's Private Cabinets
18. The King's Apartment*
19. The Queen's Apartment
20. The Queen's Private Cabinets*
a. The Queen's Staircase
21. Mme de Maintenon's Apartment*
b. Coronation Room
c. Room 144
d. 1792 Room
22. 1830 Room

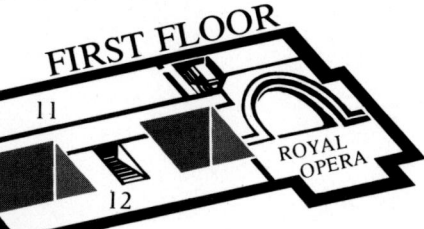

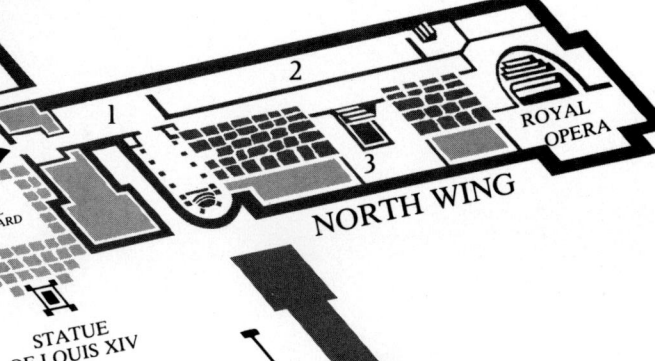

THE ENTRANCE COURTYARDS

A. Main Gateway
B. Ministers' Wings
C. Museum Entrance
D. Path leading to Gardens
D* Entrance to Gardens when the Great Fountains are in play
E. Marble Courtyard

PLAN OF THE CHATEAU

THE CHATEAU

THE ENTRANCE COURTYARDS

After passing through the main gateway crowned with the arms of France, the visitor crosses the Great Courtyard, flanked to the north and south by two long brick and stone wings called the Ministers' Wings.

The great equestrian statue of Louis XIV was placed here by Louis-Philippe.

Beyond lies the Royal Courtyard, once separated from the Great Courtyard by a railing. Only those lords who had the right to the "Honours of the Louvre" were able to enter it by carriage. This courtyard is lined to the right by the Gabriel Wing, a remainder of Louis XV's plans to reconstruct the château, and to the left by the Old Wing, built in 1662. Its end section was rebuilt in the early 19th century to match the Gabriel Wing.

Next come two small wings with gilded entrances leading, on the left, to the Queen's Staircase and, on the right, to the vestibule of the former Ambassadors' Staircase.

Finally, there is the Marble Courtyard, which is being raised to its former level. The surrounding brick and stone façades trace the outline of the small château built by Louis XIII in 1631.

The Royal Courtyard, Gabriel Wing and Chapel

THE 17TH CENTURY ROOMS

After crossing the entrance hall, called the Gabriel Vestibule, and the lower Chapel Vestibule, one begins the tour of the château by the rooms on the ground-floor and the first floor of the north wing on the side overlooking the gardens. These rooms were once the Princes' apartments, destroyed when Louis-Philippe had the château of Versailles transformed into a museum. They are now devoted to a display of 17th century iconography and in this way serve as an introduction to the history of the château and the tour of its apartments.

Naturally, the reign of Louis XIII begins these galleries; next come various portraits of Louis XIV, the Princes and Princesses of his family, views of the former royal châteaux, military scenes by Van der Meulen or his pupils and large works portraying important events of the reign, all of which gradually create around the visitor the atmosphere and history of the *Grand Siècle*. A large number of works by artists of the Académie royale, whose talent contributed to the Sun King's magnificence, are also displayed here.

In the last room before the upper Chapel Vestibule, a large tapestry cartoon, representing the audience granted by Louis XIV to the Doge of Genoa at Versailles on 15th May 1685, shows the King in the Hall of Mirrors still adorned with the silver furniture which was unfortunately to be melted down in 1689.

Not all the works displayed here can be considered equal in quality; however, here, as in the rest of the museum, an effort has been made to display only sculptures and paintings created at the same time as the events portrayed.

First floor of the 17ᵗʰ century rooms

The Viscounte de Turenne by Le Brun

THE ROYAL CHAPEL

Dedicated to Saint Louis, the ancestor of the Kings of France, this is the fifth chapel to have been built in the château of Versailles. The former chapels lacked the majesty of this one and very quickly proved to be too small. It was not until 1699 that new plans were presented by Hardouin-Mansart, whose brother-in-law, Robert de Cotte, completed the building in 1709.

Situated near the north wing, it was constructed according to the traditional two-storeyed gothic chapels (like the Sainte Chapelle in Paris). Here, however, tradition was adapted to the classical style. The whole decoration stresses the parallel between the Old and New Testaments, in particular, in the ceiling paintings, the work of Jouvenet, Coypel and La Fosse, which evoke the doctrine of the Trinity, or the relief adorning the organ-loft (above the altar), portraying King David. The side chapels are dedicated to the various patron saints of the royal family and many were not decorated until the time of Louis XV. The chapel of the Sacred Heart, created by Gabriel behind the high altar, also dates from the reign of this King.

Since this chapel was consacrated only on 5th June 1710 by Cardinal de Noailles, it was not here that the principal religious ceremonies of Louis XIV's life at Versailles took place. However, from this time on, besides the daily masses or ceremonies of the Order of the Holy Spirit, all the baptisms and marriages of the Children of France and the Princes of the Blood were celebrated here : among the most interesting marriages to take place here were the two successive marriages of the Dauphin, Louis XV's son, in 1745 and 1747, and the marriage of the future Louis XVI to Archduchess Marie-Antoinette in 1770.

Between 1710 and 1789, a great number of Te Deums were sung here as well, to celebrate royal victories or births. Normally, the King and Queen sat in the first floor gallery, opposite the altar, where a Savonnerie carpet, delivered in 1760, has been returned.

THE UPPER CHAPEL VESTIBULE

The upper Chapel Vestibule, which links the royal gallery to the State Apartments, is a large drawing-room with a marble floor, its walls decorated with stone and, in two niches, the figures of "Glory holding Louis XV's medallion", by Vassé, and "Royal Magnanimity", by Bousseau.

The Royal Chapel, the high altar

The upper Chapel Vestibule

THE HERCULES ROOM

On the first floor of the château, on the site where the fourth chapel stood from 1682 to 1710, this room lies at the junction of the central section and the north wing. Its decoration was begun in 1712 by Robert de Cotte, who wanted to create a setting worthy of the masterpiece by Veronese, "The Meal at the House of Simon", given to the King by the Venetian Republic. Interrupted by the death of Louis XIV in 1715, work was resumed in 1725 and completed from 1733 to 1736 with the extraordinary painted ceiling by François Lemoine portraying "The Apotheosis of Hercules". The same god was carved in bronze by Vassé on the mantelpiece of the monumental fireplace above which hangs another painting by Veronese: "Eliezier and Rebecca".

This drawing-room, the largest in the château, was not only a passage for the King on his way to chapel but also a ballroom or audience chamber: in 1739, for the great ball held by Louis XV (at this ball full Court attire was worn and each dancer had his specially defined place); in 1769, for the *grand couvert* for the marriage of the Duc de Chartres; in 1789, for the presentation of the deputies of the Estates-General to the King.

The Hercules Room

PLAN OF THE 1st FLOOR OF THE CHATEAU

THE QUEEN'S APARTMENT

8. Peace Drawing-Room
9. Queen's Bedchamber
10. Room of the Queen's Gentlemen
11. The *"Grand Couvert"* Antechamber
12. Guard Room
13. Queen's Staircase
14. Loggia

* THE QUEEN'S PRIVATE CABINETS

a. Bathchamber
b. Library Annexe
c. Gilded Cabinet
d. Gilded Library
e. The Meridian Cabinet
f. Duchess de Bourgogne's former Cabinet

* THE APARTMENT OF MADAME DE MAINTENON

g.-h. Antechambers
i. Bedchamber
j. State Cabinet

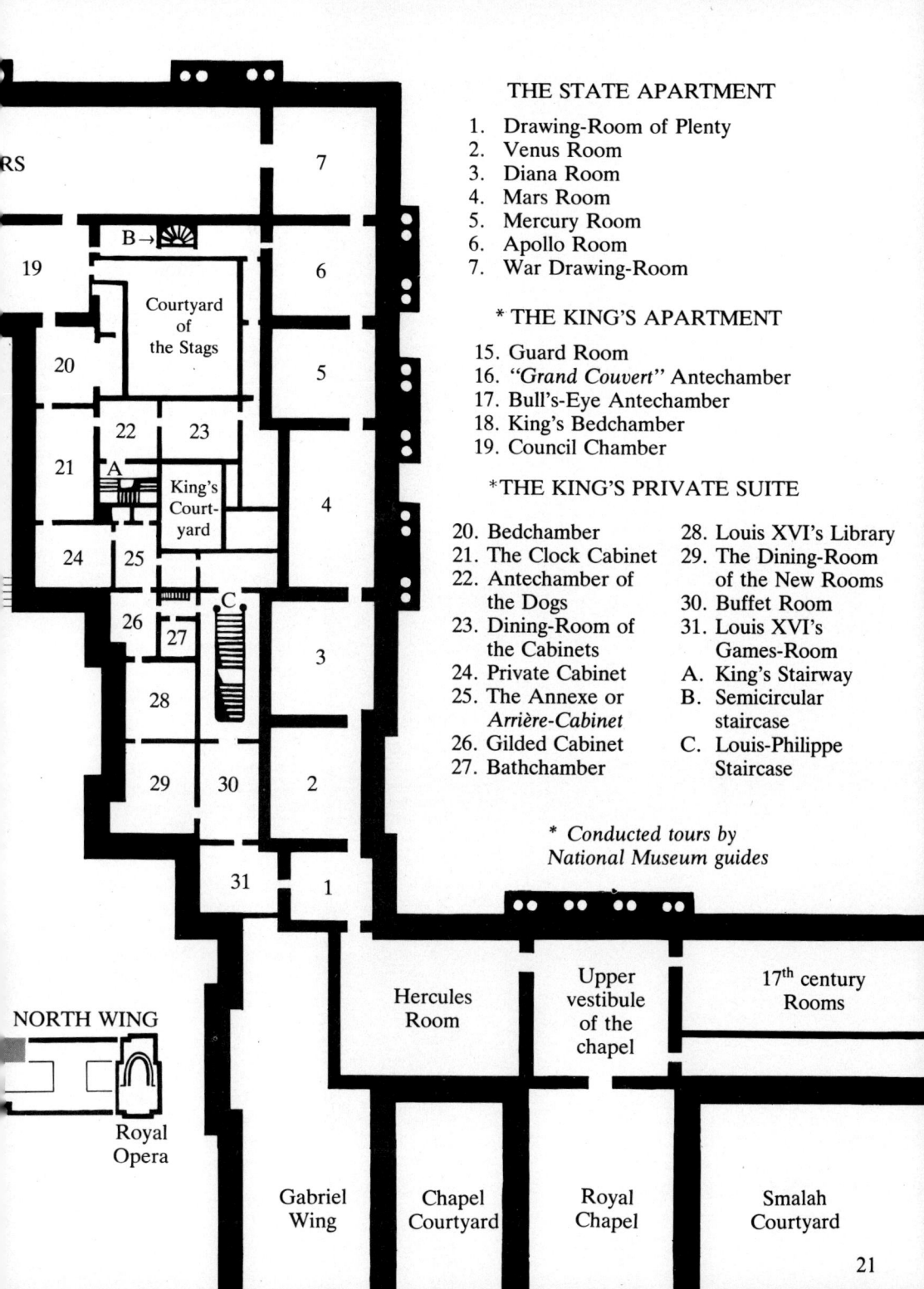

The series of drawing-rooms in the State Apartment

THE STATE APARTMENT

This is the name given to the suite of rooms which occupy the first floor of the northern end of the château's central section and also overlook the park.

The decoration was supervised by Charles Le Brun. This suite underwent several changes : from 1673 to 1682 it effectively contained the King's Apartments with a guard room (Mars Room), antechamber (Mercury Room) and bedchamber (Apollo Room); then followed the Cabinets which were removed to make way for the War Drawing-Room and Hall of Mirrors.

When Louis XIV made Versailles the seat of government in 1682, he had a new apartment created around the Marble Courtyard. This apartment was enlarged after the Queen's death in 1683.

From that time on, the State Apartment, which one reached via the Ambassadors' Staircase and the Venus and Diana Rooms, was reserved for Court ceremonies and the special form of entertainments held on Mondays, Wednesdays and Thursdays. These festivities were called "apartment" evenings.

Very rapidly, the perfect décor of these rooms acquired such widespread renown that it was never thought of changing it, even

when plans were made to alter the château in the 18th and 19th centuries.

Since the paintings by the old masters and the precious fabrics which once covered these walls could not be returned to their original settings, they have been replaced by Gobelins tapestries relating the History of the King and by Savonnerie carpets portraying the pomp and splendour of the *Ancien Régime*. The furniture in these rooms consisted in the main of benches, stools, tables and candlestands and the fabrics were changed according to the seasons.

THE DRAWING-ROOM OF PLENTY

Once the vestibule of the chapel when it occupied the site of what is now the Hercules Room, the Drawing-Room of Plenty also opened onto the Cabinet of Curios and Rare Objects (today Louis XVI's Games Room). The ceiling, by Houasse, depicts "Royal Munificence" and the room was named after some of the finest pieces in the sovereign's collections, placed on a false, painted balustrade; these pieces inspired the décor of this room.

On "apartment" evenings, the room was used for serving drinks : "Three large buffets stand along three sides of this room. The one in the middle... is for hot drinks such as coffee, chocolate etc. The other two buffets are for liqueurs, sherbets and the juice of various fruits".

Today, green Genoan velvet gallooned with a gold fringe covers the walls decorated with portraits of royalty. Medal-cabinets, built after designs by Boulle, and classical busts from the royal collections call to mind the luxury of this first room in the State Apartment.

The Drawing-Room of Plenty

THE VENUS ROOM

Like the following room, dedicated to Diana, the Venus Room served as the upper vestibule to the Ambassadors' Staircase until the middle of Louis XV's reign (1752). Like the Diana Room, its marble décor has remained completely intact, setting into relief, in a niche opposite the windows, a statue of Louis XIV, by Jean Warin.

The name of Venus, the first deity in the mythological cycle decorating the State Apartment, was given to this room because of the ceiling, by Houasse, depicting "the goddess of love subjugating the Gods and Powers". The corners represent famous lovers of Antiquity. However, it is the murals which particularly attract our attention, with two *trompe-l'œil* statues of "Meleager" and "Atalanta" between the windows and, on the side walls, paintings of false perspectives. All these are the work of the artist Jacques Rousseau.

On "apartment" evenings, the room was "lined with tables with (light refreshments)... As these refreshments were intended to be partaken of in their entirety, they remained there for the four hours during which the entertainments took place, and everyone chose and took what was most to his taste".

Door to the Ambassadors' Staircase

*The Venus Room
Louis XIV, by Jean Warin*

*The Diana Room,
Bust of Louis XIV, by Bernini*

THE DIANA ROOM

This room is dedicated to Apollo's sister, Diana, goddess of night, depicted by Blanchard in the centre of the ceiling " as she presides over hunting and navigation ". These themes were picked up in the covings where Audran painted " Cyrus hunting boar", on the left, and " Caesar sending a Roman colony to Carthage " on the far wall. Above the window is La Fosse's work, " Alexander hunting lions" while "Jason and the Argonauts" by the same artist is in the cove near the fireplace and "Diana rescuing Iphigenia" hangs over the fireplace. Opposite, Blanchard shows the goddess watching over Endymion in his slumber. Against the central wall, as the climax to this marble décor which has remained intact for three centuries, stands the bust of Louis XIV, by Bernini. Eight classical busts with marble or porphyry heads accompany that of the King. A bas-relief by Sarrazin, depicting the "Flight into Egypt", has been set into the chimneypiece. The Diana Room was originally used as a Billiards Room. The billiard-table, covered with gold-fringed, crimson velvet, stood in the centre of the room. The ladies of Court could follow the game, at which the Great King excelled, from carpeted platforms along the walls.

Above the fireplace
Diana saving Iphigenia

THE MARS ROOM

The cornice adorned with helmets and war trophies is a reminder of the time when this room served as a Guard Room. In the centre of the ceiling is the God of War, painted by Audran. At the time of Louis XIV, the fireplace was flanked by two galleries for the musicians who played on "apartment" evenings, for the Mars Room, after being used as a Games Room, was transformed into a concert hall or ballroom on these occasions.

The galleries were removed under Louis XV. It was during his reign that the two great portraits of the King and Queen by Van Loo were hung here. While the portrait of Maria Leczinska was able to be returned, that of Louis XV was replaced by another portrait of the sovereign, painted by Rigaud. Domenichino's "David playing the Harp", which can be seen over the fireplace, hung in the King's bedchamber under the *Ancien Régime*.

During the reign of Louis XIV, the furniture included two immense marquetry cabinets; mention is later made of eighteen benches, upholstered with crimson silk, and two large mirrors, placed between the windows, which reflected the sumptuous light-fittings.

The tapestries illustrating the History of the King replace the paintings by Veronese, Mignard and Le Brun which, according to the season, once adorned the wall opposite the windows.

The two porphyry vases were already in this room under the *Ancien Régime*.

The Mars Room

THE MERCURY ROOM

There is, unfortunately, no remnant in this room of the dazzling luxury of its décor when it was Louis XIV's state bedchamber. The walls were covered with panels of brocade, the bed with very richly embroidered fabrics. It was separated from the rest of the room by a silver balustrade. The rest of the furniture was also made of silver, from the table and ten-foot high mirror between the windows to the andirons, candelabra and chandeliers. It was all melted down in 1689. However, the ceiling, painted by Jean-Baptiste de Champaigne, still remains, as does the automaton clock given to Louis XIV by Antoine Morand in 1706 and immediately placed in this room, which the King had stopped using as a bedchamber. The Mercury Room was, nevertheless, used as a chamber on a number of occasions: in 1700, by the Duc d'Anjou, who had become King of Spain under the name of Philip V; in 1701, by the King himself, while his new bedchamber was being completed; in 1715, when, after his death, his coffin was displayed here before being taken to Saint-Denis. Two chests-of-drawers, executed by Boulle in 1708, are worth noticing : they were once part of Louis XIV's furniture in the Grand Trianon.

The threshold of the Mercury Room

THE APOLLO ROOM

The drawing-rooms in the State Apartment end with the Apollo Room, the most sumptuous of all. It was dedicated to the King's symbol, the Sun. In the centre of the ceiling painted by Charles de La Fosse one can see "Apollo in his chariot accompanied by the seasons".

In this room stood the throne, adorned with gold-embroidered velvet in winter and gold and silver brocade in summer. The back of the throne was eight and a half feet high and was surmounted by a canopy embellished with a figure of Fame. This throne, originally carved in silver, was replaced in 1689 by a similar one of gilded wood and was later renovated during the reign of Louis XV.

It was in this room that the sovereign granted his official audiences, the state audiences being held in the Hall of Mirrors. On "apartment" evenings, however, Louis XIV, who, like his father, Louis XIII, was very musical, devoted the Apollo Room to music and, in 1683, Abbé Bourdelot related that "(the King) was not seated on his throne; there were three cushions on the edge of the dais; I was astonished to see him sitting there quite simply... I admired the airs that His Majesty ordered to be sung; (...) here, among those he knows, he is accessible to all."

Nowadays, a tapestry marks the site where the throne once stood. It is framed by two others from the History of the King series depicting the Audiences Granted by Louis XIV. Above the fireplace hangs a painting of the monarch himself, by Rigaud. Opposite is the portrait of Louis XVI, also in royal robes, by Callet.

The ceiling of the Apollo Room

The War Drawing-Room

THE WAR DRAWING-ROOM

This drawing-room is situated at the end of the King's State Apartment but does not, however, belong to it. With the Hall of Mirrors and the Peace Drawing-room, it forms the most famous set of rooms on the first floor of the central section. Mansart began building it in 1678 and, in 1686, Le Brun completed its décor which celebrates the military victories which led to the Treaty of Nimeguen. The central ceiling painting depicts "France armed" with a portrait of Louis XIV adorning her shield.

The paintings in the coves portray the allied powers: Germany on her knees with her eagle at her side, Spain, threatening, with her lion, Holland lying on the lion of Flanders and, in the fourth arching, Bellona, the goddess of War, with Rebellion and Discord on either side.

The décor of the walls is entirely of marble, with bronze trophies which were completed only in 1701. On the wall between this and the Apollo Room is a large, oval, stucco bas-relief, by Coysevox, representing Louis XIV crossing a battlefield on horseback. Above this famous work hover two figures of Fame. The carving is supported by two chained captives, also the work of Coysevox, as is the bas-relief, "Clio writing the History of the King".

THE HALL OF MIRRORS

Until 1678, a simple terrace occupied this site. Louis XIV commissioned Mansart to build a gallery, decorated by Le Brun and completed in 1686. It is lit by seventeen windows matched by seventeen mirror-archways. The niches between the pilasters held some of the finest classical sculptures in the royal collections, several of which have been returned to their original settings. In 1689, the candlestands, vases and silver tables which decorated the gallery were replaced by a suite of gilt-wood furniture which was renovated a number of times, particularly from 1769 to 1770. This 1770 suite is the one which was able to be restored.

The Hall of Mirrors was used as a passage. Each day, the courtiers would wait here for the King and the royal family on their way to mass in procession. It was also the setting for receptions held for ambassadors or for state audiences. Throughout the entire reigns of Louis XV and Louis XVI, balls were given here in honour of royal marriages. After the Revolution, great events once more took place here, such as the proclamation of the German Empire on 18th January 1871 or, on 28th June 1919, the signing of the Treaty of Versailles, which put an end to the First World War.

The Hall of Mirrors

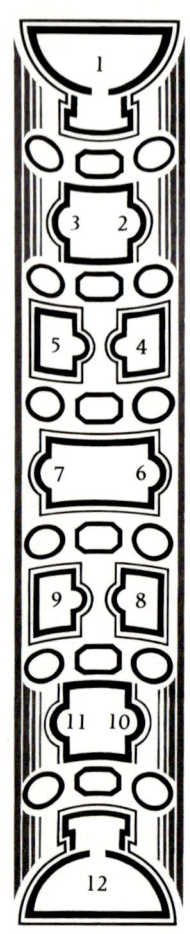

WAR DRAWING-ROOM

PEACE DRAWING-ROOM

Themes of the nine large paintings on the ceiling from the War Drawing-Room to the Peace Drawing-Room :

1. Alliance of Germany and Spain with Holland, 1672.
2. Crossing the Rhine in the presence of the enemy, 1672.
3. The King takes Maestricht in thirteen days, 1673.
4. The King giving orders to attack four of Holland's strongholds at the same time, 1672.
5. The King arming his fleet and his army, 1672.
6. The King governs alone, 1661.
7. Pomp of France's neighbouring powers.
8. Franche-Comté conquered a second time, 1674.
9. Resolution passed to make war on the Dutch, 1674.
10. Capture of the city and citadel of Ghent in six days, 1678.
11. *Spanish action destroyed by the capture of Ghent.
12. Holland accepts peace and breaks with Germany and Spain, 1678.

Ceiling of the Hall of Mirrors : detail from the central painting

The Peace Drawing-Room

THE QUEEN'S APARTMENT

All the Queens and several Dauphines lived in this suite, situated at the south end of the central section on the first floor. It consists of a guard room, two antechambers, a bedchamber and a games room, which is none other than the Peace Drawing-Room, by which the tour of this apartment begins.

THE PEACE DRAWING-ROOM

This room matches the War Drawing-Room perfectly. However, as one might expect, the ceiling, also by Le Brun, portrays "the apotheosis of France, the bringer of peace", while the covings contain paintings of the same countries as the War Drawing-Room; this time, however, they are shown at peace with one another. The walls are also decorated in marble and bronze. The painting over the fireplace was not hung here until 1729; the work of Lemoine, it depicts "Louis XV bestowing peace on Europe".

At the end of Louis XIV's reign, the Peace Drawing-Room was made part of the Queen's Apartment for the Dauphine de Bourgogne. From then on it was the Queen's games room. Later, Maria Leczinska, Louis XV's wife, created the custom of holding concerts of sacred or secular music here each Sunday.

A partition was then erected to fill the arch between this room and the Hall of Mirrors and Marie-Antoinette had a small theatre created against this wall to pass the time while awaiting the birth of her first child.

THE QUEEN'S BEDCHAMBER

The bedchamber we see today was redecorated in 1729 for Maria Leczinska. Work was directed by Gabriel and completed in 1735. The monochrome ceiling paintings, by Boucher, and the overdoors, by Natoire and De Troy, match Verberckt's carved wood-panelling. In 1770, the two-headed eagle of the House of Austria was added to the archings for Marie-Antoinette. On becoming Queen, she had the tapestry portraits of Louis XVI, her mother, Empress Maria-Theresa, and her brother, Joseph II, placed above the mirrors in 1775. She ordered the present fireplace to be placed here in 1783. The summer wall-hanging, commissioned in 1786, was rewoven. It was here on the Queen's last night at Versailles, on 5th October 1789. The canopy over the bed and a balustrade were carved as they had once been. Schwerdfeger's jewellery-cabinet, the firescreen and the andirons have been returned to this room, as has the wall-clock between the windows. The Queen spent a large part of her life here. Each morning she granted her private audiences. In this bedchamber two Queens and two Dauphines died and nineteen Children of France were born.

The Queen's Bedchamber

THE ROOM OF THE QUEEN'S GENTLEMEN

The Queen granted her audiences here and had the ladies recently admitted to Court presented to her. On these occasions, the sovereign's chair was placed on a dais opposite the windows, beneath a canopy supported by two bolts still in the cornice to this day.

However, it was here, too, that the coffins of the Queens and Dauphines who had died in the adjoining room were displayed. From 18th to 23rd February 1712, an unceasing flow of people came to pay respect to the bodies of the Dauphin and Dauphine, Louis XV's parents.

It was also in this room that the Queen generally received her ladies-in-waiting and that each morning the nobles would wait to meet her after her rising ceremony; (for this reason the room was called the Room of the Queen's Gentlemen).

Of the original décor, only the ceiling, painted by Michel Corneille for Marie-Thérèse, remains. All the rest was renovated for Marie-Antoinette in 1785 on the birth of her second son, (the future Louis XVII). The fireplace, the chests-of-drawers and corner cupboards by Riesener and the large Gobelins tapestry portrait of Louis XV date from her time.

*The Room of
the Queen's Gentlemen*

THE QUEEN'S ANTECHAMBER

The ceiling adorned with war motifs is a reminder of the time when this large room was Marie-Thérèse's Guard Room, before becoming an antechamber when the Dauphine, Maria-Anna of Bavaria, her daughter-in-law, moved into the apartment of the Queens.

The footmen stood here night and day and visitors would wait here before being granted an audience. This antechamber was also used from early on for plays or concerts and this is how, during one of the Dauphine de Bourgogne's pregnancies, Corneille's "Polyeucte" and "The Misanthropist", by Molière, came to be put on here. Marie-Antoinette later had a gallery erected for her musicians against the wall between this and the adjoining Guard Room.

This room is also called the *Grand Couvert* Antechamber, for it was here that the King and Queen dined in public: "to the joy of the provincial visitors who, after having watched (the Queen) eat her soup, would go to see the princes eat their boiled meat and then run till they were out of breath to watch Mesdames eat their desert." Almost all of the original décor of this room was able to be reconstituted, except for the centre of the ceiling which once portrayed the god Mars, and was replaced during the 19th century by an old replica of "Darius' Tent", by Le Brun.

Above the fireplace hangs the famous painting, by Madame Vigée-Lebrun, of Marie-Antoinette with her three children, the Dauphin, Madame Royale and the Duc de Normandie.

The Queen's Antechamber

The Room of the Queen's Guard

THE ROOM OF THE QUEEN'S GUARD

A chapel until 1676, this room then became the Room of the Queen's Guard. Its marble décor, completed in 1681, has remained intact, as has the ceiling, by Noël Coypel, portraying Jupiter. Coypel repeated the Jupiter theme in two other paintings, one above the fireplace, the other on the opposite wall. The overdoors in this room are not paintings but gilt-metal bas-reliefs by Le Gros and Massou.

This room was constantly cluttered with racks for the guards' arms and screen hiding their camp-beds. Here, the ladies of Court, with the exception of the Princesses of the Blood, would leave their sedan-chairs before going to see the Queen.

A number of important events took place in this room and the King held several "Beds of Justice" here; on such occasions, in his presence, the Paris Parliament had no choice but to bow to the decisions of royalty.

On 6th October 1789, the mob which had been trying to invade the château met with the heroic resistance of the guards in this room. Their devotion gave the Queen time to seek refuge in the King's Apartment.

The Coronation of Napoleon I, by David

THE CORONATION ROOM

This room, now the Coronation Room, was formerly the Great Guard Room for both the King and Queen and replaced the château's third chapel in 1682.

Each Holy Thursday, the King would wash the feet of thirteen children of the poor here, have a meal served for them and give them a purse containing thirteen *écus*.

When Louis-Philippe transformed the château of Versailles into a museum, he devoted this immense room to the Empire by having three large works hung here: "The Battle of Aboukir, on 25th July 1799", an immense canvas commissioned by Murat from Baron Gros in 1806, "The Army swearing loyalty to the Emperor after the Distribution of the Eagle Standards, on the Champs de Mars, 5th December 1801", by David, who completed the work in 1810, and, finally, "The Coronation of Napoleon I by Pope Pius VII on 2nd December 1804 at Notre-Dame Cathedral in Paris". The room is named after this painting. The original was moved to the Louvre at the end of the 19th century and the work here is a copy completed in exile by the same painter in 1822. The ceiling, raised by Louis-Philippe, depicts an "Allegory of 18th Brumaire", by Callet.

THE 1792 ROOM

After being the Room of the Swiss Guards under Louis XVI, this room, which links the central section of the château and the south wing, was dedicated to the year 1792 by Louis-Philippe. This year saw not only the fall of the Monarchy but also the first of the revolutionary wars in which Louis-Philippe, then still the young Duc de Chartres, won great renown. For this reason, in addition to a series of portraits of the greatest officers of these campaigns, La Fayette, Dumouriez, Kellermann, Bonaparte and Chartres himself, this room contains two paintings of the Battles of Valmy and Jemmapes and a third portraying "the Departure of the National Guard of Paris for the Army".

THE HALL OF BATTLES

On leaving the 1792 Room, one crosses the landing of a stone staircase, called the Princes' Staircase because it led to the apartments occupying the entire south wing on the gardens side and which were set aside for the Children of France and the Princes of the Blood.

It was these apartments that Louis-Philippe chose as the site for the greatest of his creations at Versailles, the Hall of Battles.

However, although this gallery won a great deal of admiration at the time of its inauguration, it cannot efface the memory of the magnificent apartments destroyed by the architects Fontaine and Nepveu to make way for this vast vessel, 394 feet long and 43 feet wide.

Here, thirty-three paintings depicting war-scenes from the Battle of Tolbiac to that of Wagram, eighty-two busts of warriors and sixteen bronze plaques bearing the names of heroes who died for France unite to conjure up the military pomp not only of the *Ancien Régime* but also of Imperial France. Louis-Philippe wished to create a symbol of national reconciliation by placing among these works an immense painting by Gérard portraying, not a battle-scene, but "Henri IV entering Paris on 22nd March 1594". This event put an end to the wars of religion and marked the victory of the Bourbons over the League. Among the finest paintings in this gallery is "The Battle of Taillebourg", by Delacroix. The 1830 Room, a continuation of the Hall of Mirrors, was intended to honour the reconciliation between the Monarchy (of Louis-Philippe) and the Revolution. (The room is at present being restored).

The 1792 Room
The Departure of the Volunteers

The Hall
of Battles

THE QUEEN'S STAIRCASE

Built between 1679 and 1681, this staircase on the Queen's Apartment side matched, to the south, the Ambassadors' Staircase which lay to the north, on the side of the King's Apartment.

Marble of different colours forms the basis of its décor. In the middle of the landing on the first floor of this staircase, two cupids hold an escutcheon bearing the King's monogram.

From 1684 on, this staircase gave access to both the Queen's and the King's apartments, for Louis XIV extended his suite to surround the Marble Courtyard. It then became the most frequently used staircase in the château. In 1701, an arcade was created in the wall on the Royal Courtyard side to open on to a vestibule which led to the Room of the King's Guard on the left and, on the right, to Madame de Maintenon's apartment.

It was at this time that the large work with false perspectives that we see today was painted on the wall opposite the real arcade.

One should keep in mind that it was via the Queen's Staircase that the revolutionary mob who had marched on Versailles from Paris invaded the château on the morning of 6th October 1789.

The Loggia of the Queen's Staircase

A trophy on the landing, "the royal monogram"

THE KING'S APARTMENT

THE ANTECHAMBERS

After the death of Marie-Thérèse in 1683, Louis XIV linked to his apartment the south section of the Marble Courtyard which, until then, had been reserved for the Queen. His State Apartment, overlooking the north parterre, became the official apartment and the King moved into these new rooms comprising a guard room, two antechambers, a bedroom and council chamber. The very simply decorated Guard Room preceded the First Antechamber, called the *Grand Couvert* Antechamber, where the King dined in public.

Then comes the Second Antechamber, or Antechamber of the King's Gentlemen, better known as the Bull's Eye Antechamber after the windows in its cornice. This room was increased to its present size in 1701, when the former Bassano Room (named after the artist whose works hung there) was joined to the bedchamber used by the King between 1683 and 1701.

"It was in the Bull's Eye Antechamber that the princes and lords would wait for him to awaken before entering his bedchamber".

The King also used this antechamber to go to the Queen's apartment.

The Bull's Eye Drawing-Room

THE KING'S BEDCHAMBER

In 1701 Louis XIV converted the State Drawing-Room in the centre of the château into his bedchamber. It was here that he died in 1715 and here, too, that one must imagine the King's famous rising and retiring ceremonies, which still took place in this room even after Louis XV had his small bedchamber created in 1738. The carved décor, with "France watching over the King in his slumber" by Coustou set over the bed, dates from the time of the Great King. He also commissioned the paintings in the wainscoting. Only the original violet brecciated marble fireplace from the time of his ancestor was removed by Louis XV in 1761 and replaced by two slate-blue marble ones.

The wall-hangings in the alcove, like the bedspread, were rewoven after a summer fabric created in 1705, restored exactly according to the original in 1723 and which remained here until 1785.

The brocade, embroidered with gold as at its creation, was rewoven at Lyons. The restoration of the King's Bedchamber took over twenty years. The chandelier, twelve folding-stools and two armchairs complete the furnishings of this room which once again exists in the dazzling splendour it knew under the monarchy of former times.

The King's Bedchamber

THE COUNCIL CHAMBER

This site originally contained two rooms: the King's Cabinet, where he held his various ministerial councils, and the Cabinet of Terms (named after the sculptures which once adorned it), where he and the Princes of his family would gather after the evening meal. The latter room also served as the Cabinet of Periwigs.

In 1755, Louis XV decided to join the two rooms to form the Council Cabinet. His architect, Ange-Jacques Gabriel, then commissioned Rousseau to carve the magnificent wood-panelling which frames the sumptuous griotte marble fireplace adorned with gilt-bronze mounts. Today, the paintings by Poussin, now in the Louvre, have been replaced by others by Houasse.

Here, for over a century, the most important decisions concerning the destiny of France were made, decisions such as the overthrow of the alliances in 1756 and, in 1775, France's participation in the American War of Independence. It was here, too, that the King granted his private audiences, signed the royal marriage contracts and received condolences or congratulations.

On several occasions, he also received the ladies from the Halles market in Paris in this room.

The Council Chamber

The King's Stairway

THE KING'S PRIVATE SUITE

Very early on, Louis XIV had a private suite created which, apart from a billiards room (on the site of the present bedchamber of Louis XV and Louis XVI), consisted of a number of cabinets where the King indulged in displaying to art-lovers some of the finest pieces in his collections.

However, we owe the present private suite to Louis XV. This sovereign very soon wanted to be able to live his private life in rooms less solemn in atmosphere that those of his ancestor. He therefore had his suite continually altered between 1738 and 1774, the year of his death, in order to ensure the greatest possible comfort. In this way, real dining-rooms were created, such as the After-Hunt Dining-Room where, as the Duc de Luynes tells us, the King would choose the guests who were to dine with him.

One may enter the private suite either via the Council Chamber or the King's stairway, by which one may also leave the apartment. This stairway was not given its final site and shape until 1754 and was extended to the second floor in 1763.

If one enters from the Council Chamber, the first room one comes to is the bedchamber, which the King had

The King's Private Suite

created in 1738; it was redecorated several times and so sumptuously furnished as to rival even Louis XIV's former chamber. Two large gold candelabra and two sugar bowls of the same metal stood on the fireplace and the chest-of-drawers opposite. It was here that the King really slept, after his public retiring ceremony. On 10th May 1774, Louis XV died here of smallpox. A small door in the alcove opens on to a dressing-room entirely redecorated in 1788 for Louis XVI. From this dressing-room, the King was able to reach the terrace overlooking the Courtyard of the Stags and thus enter the private apartments on the second floor without having to go back through his room and the private cabinets.

The beautiful, large room adjoining the bedchamber, adorned with wainscoting by Verberckt, was also transformed on several occasions and received its present décor in 1760. It is called the Clock Drawing-Room, after the large astronomical clock with a movement designed by Passemant and executed by Dauthiau. It was presented to the Academy of Sciences in 1749 and then to the King on 7th September 1750: "As a sign of His satisfaction, His Majesty commissioned a new case, to a design of His choice, created and executed by M. Caffiéri and his son."

*Louis XV's
Bedchamber*

Each year, on 31st December, the royal family would gather in the Clock Cabinet to mark the change of year shown by Passemant's clock. However, this room was also used as a Games Room and one should try to imagine the many chairs and piquet or quadrille tables with which it was furnished. The equestrian statue of Louis XV by Vassé is a small replica of the one on the Place de la Concorde by Bouchardon which was des-

*Louis XV
18th century French School*

The Clock Cabinet

troyed in 1792. The five tables with their painted stucco tops depict the royal hunts. The barometer was made in 1773 for Louis XVI while he was still Dauphin. From the Clock Cabinet one may proceed via the Antechamber of the Dogs either to the King's stairway and the After-Hunt Dining-Room or to the Private Cabinet.

It was not until 1753 that this room became an official study, after being transformed several times from 1738 onwards. In that year, the Italian griotte marble fireplace and the medal-chest by Gaudreaux were placed here. At the time they stood against the two diagonal walls after which the room was named the "Diagonal Cabinet". In 1753, the silk wall-hangings were replaced by wainscoting. Joubert created two corner cupboards in 1755 to match the medal-chest and the room was given its present appearance in 1760. It was at this time that the famous roll-top writing-desk, begun by Oeben and completed by Riesener in 1769, was commissioned. This suite of furniture remained here until 1780 and was able to be reconstructed. Beyond the Private Cabinet lies another small room called the *Arrière-Cabinet* "which served as a private study for His Majesty to keep His papers, write, draw, give orders

The King's Private Cabinet

*Mme Adélaïde,
by Nattier*

and receive His dispatches". The shelves installed in 1760 bear witness to the purpose which this room served.

THE NEW ROOMS

The New Rooms is the name given to the King's Private Cabinets which lie beyond the *Arrière-Cabinet*.

They occupy the site of two of the most beautiful creations at Versailles: the Ambassadors' Staircase and the Small Gallery. Begun in 1676, the Ambassadors' Staircase led to the King's State Apartment and was used more and more frequently as a stairway of honour on the occasion of audiences granted to ambassadors, hence its name. The Small Gallery which complemented it was created in 1684 at the expense of Madame de Montespan's apartment. It consisted of a gallery and two drawing-rooms decorated by Mignard. The King had some of his finest paintings hung here, including Da Vinci's "Mona Lisa". In 1752, Louis XV had the staircase and gallery destroyed to make way for an apartment for his daughter, Madame Adélaïde. The princess lived here until 1769, when the King took over these rooms again as an extension to his Private Suite. The first of these rooms is often called "Madame Adélaïde's Music Room". In this room, her Private Cabinet, she is said to have received the young Mozart in the winter of 1763 to 1764. Louis XV made this his Coffee Parlour in 1769 and displayed part of his gold dinner service here, after which the room was called "The Room of the King's Gold Plate". Next comes a small room, Louis XV's bathroom, for which the wainscoting was created, with its gilding of green, mat, burnished and bronze hues.

Louis XVI made this his *Très-Arrière-Cabinet* or Room of the Privy Purse, where he kept the records of his private accounts.

Madame Adélaïde's Gilded Cabinet

The Library, Gabriel's last work, was created for Louis XVI on his accession to the throne. This was without a doubt the sovereign's favourite room. Documents of the time describe him studying at a small table in the window recess. The painted Pekin fabrics with a pastoral motif set into relief the richness of the wainscoting and fireplace, originally designed for Madame du Barry's drawing-room at Fontainebleau.

The Porcelain Dining-Room was named after the exhibition of Sèvres porcelain organized by the King each year: "Everyone hurried to admire and buy. The Court gave many presents and the King would enjoy watching the porcelain being unwrapped and the crowd of buyers".

The Buffet Room which follows was disfigured under Louis-Philippe but still has one of the doors which led from the Ambassadors' Staircase to the Venus Room. From 1769 onwards, this room was also used as a Billiards Room and opens on to Louis XVI's Games Room.

The Games Room occupies the site of Louis XIV's Cabinet of Medallions or Rare Objects which one reached via the Drawing-Room of Plenty. It was given its present décor in 1775. The furniture, which was found again, (corner cupboards by Riesener and chairs by Boulard) and the gouaches by Van Blarenberghe were all here during the *Ancien Régime*.

Louis XVI's Library

Louis XVI's Games Room

MADAME DE MAINTENON'S APARTMENT
AND THE 16TH CENTURY COLLECTIONS

The loggia of the Queen's Staircase opens, to the right, on to a suite of rooms which Louis XIV had made into an apartment for his morganatic wife, Madame de Maintenon, who lived there until the sovereign's death in 1715. These rooms were then altered several times and, under Louis-Philippe, simply became part of the museum. Today, the two former antechambers are devoted to 16th century portraits, a great many of which come from the collection given to Louis XIV by Roger de Gaignières in 1711. The former bedchamber now contains portraits from the time of Henri IV and a number of gouaches of the groves of Versailles, by Cotelle, commissioned for the château of Meudon. On the wall hangs a holy-water font with a relic of the Virgin's veil from the royal collections.

Portraits of ladies at Louis XIV's Court are displayed in the last room. It was in this former State Cabinet that the royal family would gather around the King and Madame de Maintenon. It was here, too, that Racine produced "Athalie", with a cast of young ladies from the Institute of Saint-Cyr who were protected by the Great King's secret wife.

THE QUEEN'S PRIVATE CABINETS

This suite of small rooms situated behind the Queen's Apartment was never as large as the King's Private Cabinets.

The suite consisted of a very small number of rooms during the time of Marie-Thérèse but was later enlarged when the Dauphine de Bourgogne lived in the Queen's Apartment. A "night-time" apartment was then created for the Duc de Bourgogne, Louis XIV's grandson and Louis XV's father.

Later, Maria Leczinska loved to withdraw to the privacy of this suite and the number of cabinets it contained was increased to roughly that of today. Their present décor, however, dates almost entirely from the time of Marie-Antoinette who gradually had them altered to suit her taste.

In the State Cabinet, with its wainscoting of 1783 and its furniture, all of which belonged to the Crown collections, the Queen would receive not only the artists she protected, (Gluck, Madame Vigée-Lebrun), but also the creators of the latest fashions, (such as the hairstylist, Léonard, or Mlle Bertin, the milliner). The royal furniture gives an idea of the

Madame de Maintenon's State Cabinet

Maria Leczinska, by Nattier

décor the Queen knew in her time.

In addition to this State Cabinet, the private cabinets consisted of a bathroom, an after-bath retiring chamber, two libraries and a small drawing-room called the Meridian Cabinet. This small octagonal room was created in 1781 on the occasion of the birth of the first Dauphin. The room was situated so that a passage could be created behind it for the servants to use without disturbing the Queen. The table, with its petrified wood top, was part of the collections of Charles I of England and was mounted in 1770 in Viena. It was a gift to Marie-Antoinette from one of her sisters.

The Queen's Private Cabinet

The Meridian Drawing-Room

Madame de Pompadour, by Nattier

THE KING'S PRIVATE APARTMENTS

The King's private apartments surround the Courtyard of the Stags on several storeys and also lie above his Private Cabinets on the second floor. This was his private realm and it was for this reason that a large number of alterations were made throughout the reigns of Louis XV and Louis XVI. These two sovereigns had geography and physics cabinets, libraries, small workshops, dining-rooms and bathrooms created here to suit their tastes and provided accomodation for those whom they wished to have close at hand.

Louis XV, for example, after accomodating his daughter-in-law, the Dauphine of Saxony, there from 1765 to 1766, had an apartment created for his latest favourite, Madame du Barry, in a suite of rooms which had previously consisted of a dining-room and small gallery. It therefore became the custom to call this Madame du Barry's Apartment. Under Louis XVI, however, part of it was reserved for the First Gentleman of the Chamber, the Duc de Villequier.

These rooms, which overlook the Courtyard of the Stags and the Marble Courtyard, still have their décor of wainscoting painted white and gilded or shining with the fresh hues of Martin varnish. The luxury of the furniture described in palace records and which has since been scattered or lost blended intimately with the charming, refined atmosphere created here by Louis XV's last mistress (who was forced to leave this apartment suddenly on the King's death in 1774). The apartment occupied until 1750 by Madame de Pompadour still remains in the attic storey above the State Apartment. The windows open on to the North Parterre.

Madame du Barry's Apartment

THE ROYAL OPERA

Theatre and music always played an essential rôle in Court life. As early as 1685, Louis XIV wanted a large theatre built at the end of the north wing, but this project was abandoned. In 1748, Louis XV commissioned new plans from Gabriel, but the Opera was not built until 1769 for the festivities in honour of the Dauphin's marriage, (Louis XVI), to Archduchess Marie-Antoinette.

Under Gabriel, construction was completed in twenty-one months. Built entirely of wood, with an elliptical ground-plan, the theatre could be made into an immense ballroom by adding a platform to the stage. The Opera was inaugurated on 16th May 1770. The banquet held on 1st October 1789 by the Bodyguard sparked off the fury of the revolutionaries and the royal family's departure. In 1837, Louis-Philippe had the theatre painted red and gold, the fashion at the time. After the 1870 war, the National Assembly sat there and the theatre was later used by the Senate. Exemplary restoration work carried out between 1952 and 1957 has endowed the theatre with its former décor of blue and pink and its great azure curtain adorned with *fleurs-de-lis* and the royal arms embroidered in gold.

The Royal Opera

THE 18TH CENTURY ROOMS

GROUND-FLOOR OF THE CENTRAL SECTION

In his Museum of French History, Louis-Philippe devoted the ground-floor of the central section to portraits of admirals, marshals and high officers. To this end, he sacrificed the former apartments of the Dauphins of France, the Dauphine, who was Louis XVI's mother, Madame de Pompadour and Louis XV's daughters.

When the museum was first reorganized, paintings concerning the 18th century were displayed here. Today, thanks to the remaining wainscoting or that found in storage, their original appearance has been restored to some of the rooms where the Children of France lived under Louis XV and Louis XVI. In the rooms overlooking the south parterre and as far as what is known as the Lower Gallery, (the long room beneath the Hall of Mirrors), a number of apartments have been reconstituted in this way: those of the Dauphin, Louis XV's son, and of his wife, Maria-Josepha of Saxony and, in particular, the Prince's bedchamber, State Cabinet and Library and the Private Cabinet of the Princess.

The rooms after the Lower Gallery and overlooking the

The Comte d'Artois by F.-H. Drouais

north parterre are at present being restored. These were once the apartments of Mesdames Adélaïde and Victoire, Louis XV's daughters. Formerly, they had been the King's Bathing Apartment under Louis XIV and were later given to Madame de Montespan, then her children, and, during the next reign, Madame de Pompadour, but only its last décor, which remained until the Revolution, can be reconstituted.

When the Marble Courtyard has been raised to its former level, the rooms overlooking it will be restored. These include the Guard Room at the end of the King's stairway and part of the Private Apartment Marie-Antoinette had created after Madame Sophie's death in 1783.

Of course, any restoration work here can only conjure up a sense of the past. However, the many portraits by Van Loo, Nattier and Vigée-Lebrun, to name only the most famous of those in this Museum, will have a setting worthy of their quality and, with the furniture from the royal collections, will enable the visitor to imagine Court life in the 18th century.

Maria-Josepha of Saxony,
by Nattier

THE CONSULATE AND EMPIRE ROOMS

Louis-Philippe set aside an extensive part of his Museum of French History for the Consulate and Empire.

On the entire ground-floor of the south wing, in particular, were hung the great paintings commissioned by the Emperor to celebrate his reign. Painted panels depicting scenes of the past surround the canvases, a perfect example of the way in which 19th century museums displayed their works. These rooms had no sooner been restored when they were destroyed by a bomb attack in 1978.

The rooms on the second floor, parallel to the ceiling of the Hall of Battles (South Attic) and those above the Queen's Apartment (Chimay Attic) also contain works concerning the Consulate and Empire. These are mainly small and medium format paintings of great artistic and iconographic interest. Gérard's sketches, Bagetti's gouaches and the paintings of Baron Lejeune, to give only a few examples, attest to the splendour of the imperial court and retrace the development of Napoleon's epic venture, from the Italian campaigns and the Egyptian expedition to the Hundred Days and including all the battles against the European coalition.

Bonaparte at Arcole, by A.-J. Gros

Louis-Philippe and his sons, by H. Vernet

THE 19TH CENTURY ROOMS

For reasons of space, the Museum of French History ends with the fall of the Second Empire in 1870. The rooms in the North Attic, at present being restored, follow chronologically those in the South Attic. The works here evoke the reigns of Louis XVIII, Charles X, Louis-Philippe and Napoleon III. None of these sovereigns ever lived at Versailles, but all were connected with it by some event in their lives, particularly Louis-Philippe, who restored the château. A painting by Horace Vernet portrays this King leaving the Great Courtyard of Versailles on horseback accompanied by his sons. His family is also depicted in Winterhalter's portraits.

In the rooms on the first floor of the north wing, courtyard side, the Coronation of Charles X will be evoked in a large work by Gérard and the African wars will be represented by paintings as celebrated as the "Capture of the Smalah of Abd-el-Kader", by Horace Vernet.
The collections of this Museum, dedicated to all the Glories of France, will then be displayed in their entirety.

THE GARDENS

The gardens of Versailles, with their parterres, pools, sculptures and groves, form a natural complement to the château.

They were laid out by the architect-gardener, Le Nôtre, in collaboration with Le Brun and Mansart. Plans had already been designed under Louis XIII, but it was through the desire of Louis XIV that they attained the greatness and perfection of a work of art. Despite later alterations, they remain the model of the "French" garden, in which, according to classical taste, nature is subjugated to a strict design. The water supply involved monumental construction work.

Louis XV made scarcely any changes, but, under Louis XVI, the trees had to be replanted and Hubert Robert endowed the avenues with the romantic atmosphere they have today. Under the Revolution the gardens narrowly escaped destruction. During the 19th century, several statues were removed. Despite all this, however, the gardens of Versailles have, in general, retained their original appearance.

Nevertheless, although the Great Park covered 14,820 acres surrounded by 27 miles of walls under the *Ancien Régime*, it consists today of no more than 2013 acres.

The Half-Moon in the Parterre of Latona

The Elements Air, by Le Hongre

THE GREAT AXES

While Le Nôtre, the King's master gardener, retained the large axes laid out by his predecessors under Louis XIII, he increased the views they offered by adding vast expanses of water. A number of avenues parallel to the principal axes cross at several points to create various groves.

Our walk through the gardens, with the help of the itinerary suggested here, will take us to the east-west axis which extends from the château to the Grand Canal and then to the north-south axis from the Fountain of Neptune to the Lake of the Swiss Guards. The best time for a tour of the groves is when the Great Fountains are in play.

Louis XIV attached such importance to them that he himself wrote a treatise on "the manner of presenting the gardens of Versailles" which may serve as a guide to this day: "On leaving the château by the vestibule opening onto the Marble Courtyard, one reaches the terrace; one should stop at the top of the steps to take in the layout of the parterres, pools and fountains. One should then continue straight ahead to the top of the Latona Parterre and pause there to look at Latona, the lizards, slopes and statues, the Royal Avenue, Apollo, the canal and then look back at the parterre and the Château." This is, in fact, a description of the east-west axis which crosses the north-south axis at the château terrace. At the north end of the latter axis are located the North Parterre with the Pyramid Fountain, the Water Avenue, the Dragon Fountain and the Fountain of Neptune. The South Parterre, Orangery and Lake of the Swiss Guards lie at the south end. A short walk would take one to the parterres near the château. It takes at least one hour to follow the itinerary suggested for all the gardens and groves, p. 79.

NORTH-SOUTH AXIS

Fountain of Neptune p. 97

The Dragon Fountain p. 96

Water Avenue p. 95

North Parterre p. 92

Water Parterre p. 80-84

South Parterre p. 98-100

The Orangery p. 101

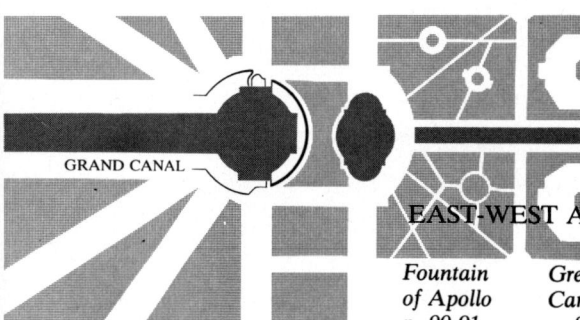

GRAND CANAL

EAST-WEST AXIS

Fountain of Apollo p. 90-91

Green Carpet p. 88-89

Fountain of Latona p. 84-87

LAKE OF THE SWISS GUARDS

The Great Fountains play from May to September, on every first and third Sunday from 4.00 p.m. to 5.00 p.m. (5.20. p.m. at the Fountain of Neptune). The fountains require about a million gallons of water (for many years pumped from the Seine by the Marly machine built in 1684).

ITINERARY FOR A TOUR OF THE GREAT FOUNTAINS

1. South Parterre
2. Orangery and Lake of the Swiss Guards
3. Water Parterre
4. Fountain of Latona
5. South Quincunx
6. Rockwork Grove
7. Queen's Grove
8. Fountain of Autumn
9. King's Garden
10. Fountain of Winter
11. Hall of Chestnut-trees
12. Colonnade
13. Green Carpet
14. Fountain of Apollo Grand Canal
15. Grove of the Domes
16. Fountain of Enceladus
17. Obelisk Fountain
18. Fountain of Spring
19. North Quincunx Star Grove
20. Fountain of Summer
21. Children's Island
22. Baths of Apollo
23. North Parterre
24. Water Avenue
25. Dragon Fountain
26. Fountain of Neptune

THE EAST-WEST AXIS

This is the main axis in the gardens, which have been laid out around a line running from the King's Bedchamber to Apollo's Chariot. This principal view begins at the terrace in front of the central section of the château, adorned with statues of the twelve months of the year surrounding those of Apollo and Diana.

At the corners of this terrace stand the War Vase, by Coysevox, and the Peace Vase, by Tubi. Four bronze statues in the classical style placed along the façade announce those in the Water Parterre where the pools reflect the entire length of the château.

The Water Parterre took on its final form between 1683 and 1690.

The statues reclining on the marble rims are the work of the finest sculptors at Versailles, Coysevox, Tubi, Le Gros, Magnier, Le Hongre, Regnaudin and bear the signatures of the Keller brothers, the founders who cast them in bronze. At the curved ends of the pools, four male and four female statues personify the various rivers of France. Eight nymphs lie along the straight edges. Children, with their joyous grace, either play beside these statues or stand in groups of three at the corners of the pools.

The Water Parterre

The decoration of the Water Parterre is completed by two slightly elevated pools at the top of the slopes which curve around the Parterre of Latona.
They are called the Fountains of the Animals and the four

The Fountain of Evening: Diana, by Desjardins

A lion bringing down a boar, by Van Clève and Raon

groups placed around their rims were cast by the Keller brothers in 1687.

These pools are surrounded by six of the finest statues commissioned in 1674. The one to the north is called the Fountain of Evening or Diana, after the nearby statue by Desjardins. On either side of Diana stand the admirable statues of Venus, by Gaspard Marsy and Air, by Le Hongre. Two lions by Van Clève and Raon struggle with a wolf and a boar.

To the south lies the Fountain of Daybreak, named after the statue by Gaspard Marsy close by. The bronzes by Houzeau represent a tiger killing a bear and a bloodhound bringing down a stag. In the foreground stand two statues, Spring or Flora, by Magnier and Water, by Le Gros.

The Fountain of Daybreak: Daybreak by Marsy

A bloodhound bringing down a stag, by Houzeau

The Lizard Fountain

The Fountain of Latona

One may descend the Latona Parterre either by the slopes lined with statues and vases or by the monumental staircase. The central fountain was created in 1670, (on the site of a pool which was already here at Louis XIII's time), and altered in 1689. We see Latona, with her children Diana and Apollo at her feet, imploring Jupiter to avenge her against the Lycian peasants who had ridiculed her. They were turned into frogs and their metamorphosis is portrayed on the three levels of this fountain and on the Lizard Fountains further on.

*The Parterre of Latona
and east-west view*

The Parterre of Latona is adorned with large vases and statues, carved from the original classical sculptures by students of the Royal Academy in Rome; they have been described as a "decorative choice made to recreate in Louis XIV's gardens (the marbles) found in the gardens of the Roman emperors." Among them there are, however, several "original works of 17th century art", such as the vases depicting the childhood of Mars, by Prou and Hardy. The most important sculptures stand at the end of the parterre, at each extremity of the staircase and on either side of the half-moon at the Royal Avenue.

The Nymph with a shell is a modern copy of the famous work by Coysevox; opposite is the Dying Gaul, a copy of the classical original. Of all these statues, only the group Castor and Pollux has remained here since Louis-XIV's time. Finally, a series of terms capture our attention by the strength or grace of their expressions.

The Half-moon in the parterre of Latona

The Parterre of Latona

The Green Carpet, a lawn slope, extends the central avenue of the Latona Parterre to the west. It already existed under Louis XIII, but it was Le Nôtre who gave it its majestic dimensions: 1099 feet in length and 210 feet wide. This is also called the Royal Avenue and is extended by the Grand Canal as far as the horizon. The central carpet of lawn is lined with two paths along which stand, in alternation, 12 marble vases and 12 statues, the majority of which were carved in the 18th century by the students of the Academy of France in Rome.

The ornamentation of these vases consists of oak or laurel leaves or sunflowers. The statues are simple allegories, for example, of cunning or constance, or represent characters from mythology or antiquity, such as the shepherd Cyparissus, Apollo's favourite. As one goes down the Royal Avenue, one will see two paths running off at right angles, with the Fountain of Saturn to the south, on the left, and that of Flora on the right, to the north. Further down, at the end of two short paths, lie the Colonnade Grove on the left and the Grove of the Domes on the other side. At the end of the Green Carpet is a half-moon, adorned with marble statues and terms, which surrounds the Fountain of Apollo.

The shepherd, Cyparissus, by Flamen

The Royal Avenue
A sunflower vase

The focal point of the east-west axis is the Apollo Fountain at the end of the Small Park. It was created in 1671 on the site of a pool which was already here during the reign of Louis XIII.

Quadrilobate in shape, it is 384 feet long and 285 feet wide. The once gilded lead group in its centre, of Apollo in his chariot, is the work of Tubi after a sketch by Le Brun. It represents daybreak, with four spirited steeds drawing the sun chariot from the sea on its journey across the sky.

Beyond lies the Grand Canal, 5118 feet long and 394 feet wide; it is intersected at its centre by an arm leading north to Trianon and south to the Menagerie (no longer in existence). Begun in 1667, it was completed in 1680. An amazing flotilla once sailed along this canal. It consisted of various small-scale reproductions of ships in the royal fleet, magnificently decorated. To this flotilla of shallops and galliots were added a number of gondolas for the Court to sail in. During festivities such as those of August 1674, a boat ride on the canal with its illuminated banks would follow a walk through the beautifully lit gardens. The gondoliers whom the King had brought from Venice were accomodated near the canal, at the spot called Little Venice to this day.

The Great Waterworks at the Fountain of Apollo

Apollo's chariot and the Grand Canal

THE NORTH-SOUTH AXIS

If one turns right on leaving the Water Parterre, one has to descend several steps to reach the North Parterre. These stairs are bordered by bronze statues: the Modest Venus, by Coysevox, and the Knife-grinder, by Foggini. A central avenue divides this parterre, with its compartments of box-tree laid out around two circular pools called the Crown Fountains. During Louis XIV's time, the groups of sirens and tritons in their centre once held large crown of *fleurs-de-lis*.

Along the palisades, at the foot of the tall trees lining the parterre to the north and west, stand several of the statues which were carved as part of the great commission of 1674 from drawings by Le Brun. They also surround the Animal Fountains and stand near the top of the Latona slopes. Most of them have

The North Parterre

been standing where we see them today since 1686. They symbolize the Four Elements, Four Parts of the Day, Four Parts of the World, Four Seasons, Four Types of Poetry and Four Temperaments. Close by the Pyramid Fountain, one will recognize one of these, the statue of Winter, a masterpiece by Girardon.

The Pyramid Fountain, at the end of the central avenue, was designed by Le Brun and executed by Girardon between 1669 and 1672. The four lead bowls are held aloft by tritons, dolphins and crayfish. These are so vividly carved that one can still easily imagine how they must have sparkled and come to life when the "silvery stream" gushed from the top of the urn and cascaded over their once gilded bodies to create what was one of the most remarkable water effects in the gardens.

Beyond this fountain, at the entrance to the Water Avenue which links the North Parterre with the Fountain of Neptune, lies the fountain of Diana's Bathing Nymphs. This is a square pool with three walls adorned with lead bas-reliefs. The most important wall, that in the centre, is the work of Girardon: "Eleven nymphs, chaste in their nakedness, splash about in the water near the bank of a river. The dream landscape is made

The Pyramid Fountain, by Girardon

almost real by the lively hues of the lead burnished by the passing of time. The sun gilds the horizon; the sky and water seem blue, the flesh tinted pink and the marine plants deep green; and, when the transparent sheet spreads over the scene, the bodies seem to quiver into life". This is the description, by Pierre de Nolhac, of one of the masterpieces in this part of the gardens at the turn of the century.

An avenue adorned with two rows of small round pools slopes away from the Bathing Nymphs. This is the Water

*South end of
the North Parterre and
the Bathing Nymphs*

Avenue or Avenue of the Marmosets. The groups of children, originally of gilt-lead, once held metal bowls adorned with flowers and fruit. The first groups, fourteen in number, were placed here in 1670. Eight more were added in 1678 and the whole set recast in bronze, with pink marble bowls, in 1688. The intertwined tritons, little dancers, cupids and satyrs in the avenue and the bird catchers in the half-moon at the end of it all express with grace the charm of childhood. At the end of the Water Avenue lies the

View of the Water Avenue from the Bathing Nymphs to the Dragon Fountain

circular Dragon Fountain, 131 feet in diameter. Children riding on swans fight a furious dragon with their bows. The main jet of water gushes from the dragon's mouth to a height of almost eighty-nine feet. The fountain's present appearance, reconstituted from drawings of long ago, dates from only 1889. Beyond, ending the park to the north, stretches the vast Fountain of Neptune, created by Le Nôtre

The Dragon Fountain

and Mansart from 1679 to 1684. It did not receive its final embellishments until the time of Louis XV, when the lead groups we see here today were placed against the retaining wall, rebuilt in 1734. Neptune and Amphitrite in the centre, carved by L.-S. Adam, are accompanied by the Ocean god on their right, sculpted by J.-P. Lemoine, and, on the left, by Proteus, the work of Bouchardon, like the two sea-dragons ridden by cupids. From these groups and from the twenty-two lead vases adorning the coping, from the channel around it and from the pool itself gush forth ninety-nine sprays of water

Fountain of Neptune: Evening Display of the Great Fountains

creating an impressive sight. In order to visit the remaining part of the north-south axis, one must return to the terrace in front of the west façade of the château's central section. One then goes to the left of the Water Parterre towards a stairway flanked by marble sphinxes carved by Lerambert to bear the bronze cupids cast by Sarrazin in 1680.

In the corner formed by the south wing and the central section, beneath the windows of the Queen's Apartment, lies the South Parterre; its main decorative element is its abundance of flowers which the gardeners renew each year at the return of the warm season. It is laid out symmetrically on either side of a central path and consists of scrolls and borders of box-tree surrounding two very simple circular pools. A marble coping runs along three sides, on which stand a set of bronze vases, initially created by Ballin, Louis XIV's goldsmith, but greatly altered during the 19th century.

The South Parterre ends, to the south, in a long stone balustrade. As we approach, we see, below, the Orangery Parterre with its majestic staircases of the Hundred Steps descending on either side.

The Orangery was built from 1684 to 1686 by Mansart. It consists of a central gallery, 504 feet long, and two lateral

The South Parterre

The South Parterre and
Lake of the Swiss Guards

The Orangery Parterre
and Lake of the Swiss Guards

ones beneath the Hundred Steps. At the time of Louis XIV, 2000 orange-trees and 1000 pomegranates and oleanders were sheltered there. Nowadays, the Orangery still contains a large number of orange-trees, oleanders and palm-trees which are brought out into the garden during the warm season.

Beyond the road to Saint-Cyr lies the Lake of the Swiss Guards, 2237 feet by 768 feet, which was dug by Louis XIV's Swiss guards from 1678 on. The equestrian statue of the King, by Bernini, was placed at its south end.

The South Wing of the château and the Orangery

THE GROVES

The itinerary on p. 79 will take us on a tour of the groves. On arriving at the end of the southern slope of the Parterre of Latona, one can see the South Quincunx adorned with eight marble terms (5). On the left a walk slopes down to the Rockwork Grove created from 1681 to 1683 and called the Ballroom "by virtue of the sort of arena on which one dances when it pleases His Majesty to hold festivities". There are steps on one side for the spectators and rockwork bowls arranged in tiers and decorated with shells (6).

The Queen's Grove dates from the time when the park was replanted under Louis XVI. Its simple shape suggests nothing of the Maze of 1673 which hid 39 fountains decorated with coloured lead animals illustrating Aesop's fables (7).

We then reach two pools dedicated to the seasons. The Fountain of Autumn is adorned with a lead group representing Bacchus, by the Marsy brothers (8). Girardon carved Saturn for the Fountain of Winter (10).

The Mirror Pool is still in its original shape. However, the following one, called the Royal Island, was replaced in the 19th century by the King's Garden (9).

To the north a path widens out to become the Hall of

The Rockwork Grove

The Fountain of Winter

Chestnut Trees (11). Its statues are a reminder of the former Hall of Classical Statues which was greatly altered in 1704.

The nearby Colonnade consists of 32 pink Languedoc, slate-blue and violet brecciated marble columns. These support a white marble cornice with spandrels depicting children's games. In 1699, Girardon's carving of the Rape of Persephone by Pluto was placed in the centre of this colonnade, constructed in 1685 by Mansart, but was later removed.

The Grove of the Domes (15) lies to the north of the Green Carpet. In its centre is a pool surrounded by a marble balustrade, around which runs a second balustrade adorned with bas-reliefs. While the statues of the end of Louis XIV's reign still surround these balustrades, only the site of the former domed pavilions remains to this day.

In the Fountain of Enceladus, a heap of rocks crushes the titan in punishment for his attempt to climb Olympus (16). A powerful spray of water rises 25 metres into the air from a clump of reeds in the centre of the pool called the Obelisk Fountain. On our way back to the château we will come to another two pools dedicated to the seasons. In the centre of the Fountain of Spring sits Flora, carved by Tubi, sur-

The Colonnade, by Mansart

The Fountain of Enceladus

rounded by cupids amongst flowers "painted according to nature" (18).

After passing the Star Grove on our left and the North Quincunx to the right (19), both of which have replaced other groves, we arrive at the Fountain of Summer for which Regnaudin carved Ceres crowned with ears of corn. Close to the Green Ring which lies on the site of the former Water Theatre (21), is a group of children, carved by Hardy, playing on a rock in a small pool.

The Grove of Apollo's Baths, created in 1778 by the painter Hubert Robert, is a romantic garden where, on the edge of a small lake, a grotto shelters the statues of Apollo tended by the Nymphs, by Girardon, and the Sun Horses, carved between 1672 and 1677 by Marsy and Guérin for the Grotto of Tethys (destroyed in 1685).

The Fountain of Spring

TRIANON

THE GRAND TRIANON

The Grand Trianon is one of a number of small châteaux built around Versailles by Louis XIV. He had already bought a village called Trianon in 1668 where, in 1670, Le Vau erected a pavilion adorned with blue and white china tiles, and therefore called the Porcelain Trianon. When it began to deteriorate seriously in 1687, it was demolished and Mansart was commissioned to construct a veritable château called the "Marble Trianon" because of its external décor of Languedoc marble pilasters. This new château, (named the Grand Trianon since the 18th century, in contrast to the Small Trianon), comprises a "peristyle" linking two front sections and two wings. At the end of the right wing and perpendicular to it is a gallery, from which another wing, called Trianon-in-the-Woods, runs off at right angles.

The interior was altered on several occasions between 1688 and 1715. After having lived in the left wing, the King let his son, the Grand Dauphin, move there in 1703 and had an apartment furnished for himself in the right front section, which once contained a small theatre.

The Grand Trianon or "Marble Trianon"

TOUR OF
THE GRAND TRIANON

1. The Mirror Drawing-Room
2. The Empress's Bedchamber
3. The Chapel Antechamber
4. The Courtiers' Drawing-Room
5. The Peristyle
6. The Round Room
7. The Music Room
8. Louis-Philippe's Family Drawing-Room
9. The Malachite Drawing-Room 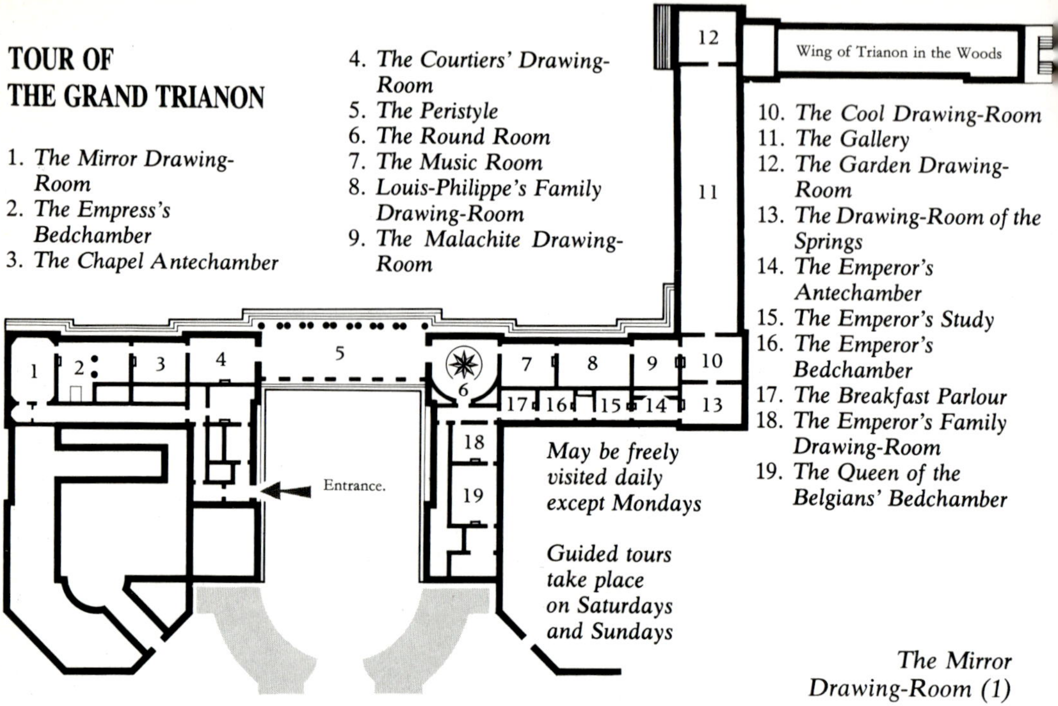
10. The Cool Drawing-Room
11. The Gallery
12. The Garden Drawing-Room
13. The Drawing-Room of the Springs
14. The Emperor's Antechamber
15. The Emperor's Study
16. The Emperor's Bedchamber
17. The Breakfast Parlour
18. The Emperor's Family Drawing-Room
19. The Queen of the Belgians' Bedchamber

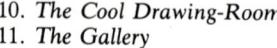
Wing of Trianon in the Woods

Entrance.

May be freely visited daily except Mondays

Guided tours take place on Saturdays and Sundays

The Mirror Drawing-Room (1)

In the right wing, reception rooms, and apartments for the Duchesse de Bourgogne and Madame de Maintenon were created. Trianon-in-the-Woods, altered in 1705, contained the apartments of the Princes and Princesses.

The finest artists worked on the construction of this château. Although the furniture (except for two chests-of-drawers by Boulle) has gone, the wood-panelling remains; (apart from the mirror and picture frames, it was never gilded). During the recent restoration of

The Empress's Bedchamber (2)

The Peristyle (5)

The Round Room (6)

Trianon, most of the paintings were able to be returned to their original settings. Among these, one should point out those in the Gallery. The work of Cotelle and Martin, they depict the gardens of Versailles in the 17th century.

Louis XIV stayed several times at Trianon, but Louis XV did so less and less often. After the visit of the Czar, Peter the Great, the château was given to Stanislas Leczinski, father of the Queen, who lived in Madame de Maintenon's apartment.

The King had this altered for himself and Madame de Pompadour and transformed Louis XIV's apartment into a games room, dining-room and buffet room.

The Grand Trianon was once more abandoned when the Small Trianon was built but was used under Louis XVI as an "annexe" for the Children of France to live in. Madame Sophie, the daughter of Louis XVI and Marie-Antoinette, died there in 1787.

Under the Revolution, the furniture was scattered but the building remained intact. On his accession to the throne, Napoleon I had the Grand Trianon restored and initially intended it for Madame Mère, whose apartment was to be situated in the left wing. Later, after his marriage to the Archduchess Marie-Louise, the Emperor kept the Grand Trianon for

Louis-Philippe's Family Drawing-Room (8)

himself, when he was thinking of having Versailles renovated to make it his residence. The peristyle was then enclosed by glass windows. The Empress lived in the left wing and Napoleon in the former apartments of Louis XV and Madame de Pompadour. The State Apartments continued to be used as such. During the Restoration, Trianon was rarely lived in, but Charles X held his last ministerial council there in 1830, before going into exile. Louis-Philippe, the citizen King, often stayed at Trianon while Versailles was being transformed into a museum. He lived with Queen Marie-Amélie in the left wing and

The Music Room (7)

its outhouses, and, in the right wing, created a large Family Drawing-Room. During his reign, his many children lived at Trianon, the Princesses in the Emperor's former apartment and the Princes and their wives in

The Malachite
Room (9)

The Gardens of Versailles in the 17th century, by Martin

Trianon-in-the-Woods. It was for Princess Marie's marriage to Duke Alexander of Württemberg that he had a chapel built in 1837 on the site of Louis XIV's billiards room. In 1845, an apartment was created in the right front section for Princess Louise and her husband, Leopold I, the King of the Belgians. Under the Second Empire, the Grand Trianon was once

more abandoned. After the war of 1870, the peristyle was converted into a court of law for the trial of Marshal Bazaine, presided over by the Duc d'Aumale, Louis-Philippe's son. In 1910, this peristyle was restored to its Louis XIV state and the peace treaty with Hungary was signed in the Gallery in 1920.

However, for lack of upkeep, the château was threatened with decay. General de Gaulle's desire to use it for visits by foreign Heads of State

The Drawing-Room of the Springs (13)

The Gardens of Versailles in the 17th century, by Martin

The Emperor's Bedchamber (16)

therefore came just in time and led to the restoration of both the exterior and interior. Almost all the 17th century paintings were able to be returned to their original places, but it was impossible to find the furniture of the *Ancien Régime*. On the other hand, nearly all the furniture of the Empire was still in existence and has been returned to the rooms for which its creators, artists such as Jacob-Desmalter or Marcion, had intended it. (One should notice, in particular, the magnificent furniture with malachite tops in the Emperor's State Cabinet).

The carpets and silks were able to be rewoven according to the originals, of which designs and samples still existed. The rooms created by Louis-Philippe were restored as he had designed them. Any missing furniture was replaced by similar pieces from châteaux no longer remaining today, such as Saint-Cloud and Meudon.

GRAND TRIANON GARDENS

The Upper Garden consists of two large parterres filled with flowers. To the east, a stairway separates it from the Lower Garden where Louis XIV had orange-trees and fragrant shrubs placed. A terrace to the south overlooks the Horseshoe Pool. Various other pools with

The Cascade

fairly simple lead embellishments serve as mirrors for the parterres or, like the "Ceiling" or *Rondeau*, reflect the trees in a glade. Mythological subjects are rare here. The Cascade, however, is a marble fountain with motifs drawn from the theme of Neptune and Amphitrite. To the north, the grove called the Hall of Classical Statues surrounds a pool with a group by Hardy. The little faun at the Pool with two Half-Moons was carved by Marsy. Finally, while the Garden of Springs has become a simple lawn, the King's Garden is still adorned with its parterres of floral embroidery.

The Upper Garden in front of the "Peristyle"

THE SMALL TRIANON

To the east of the Grand Trianon, Louis XV had new gardens laid out to cover the whole estate of the Small Trianon. He had an extraordinary botanical garden created there by Jussieu and Richard. Its exotic trees are today the glory of the Jardin des Plantes in Paris, where they were transferred by Louis XVI. In addition, a menagerie was built by Gabriel from 1749 to 1753, but also destroyed during the following reign.
In 1750, Louis XV, wishing

*The Small Trianon
Staircase*

to use his new estate to its fullest advantage, had a small pavilion erected, where he could rest and take refreshments. This is called the French Pavilion, which consists of a central drawing-room surrounded by four smaller ones. Before it lies the French Garden. As he came to like Trianon more and more, Louis XV wanted a small château, which Gabriel built in the axis of this garden between 1762 and 1768. The Small Trianon has a square ground-plan with a basement (visible only from the main courtyard and the Temple of Love), a main floor and an attic storey. Each façade is different; the most richly ornamented, with its portico of columns and two flights of stairs, overlooks the French Garden.

To the left of the main courtyard lie the chapel and outhouses. Originally intended for Madame de Pompadour's pleasure, the Small Trianon was inaugurated by Madame du Barry. There, at the end

The Small Trianon Dining-Room

Marie-Antoinette's
Theatre (3)

of April 1774, Louis XV was struck down by smallpox and had to be moved to Versailles, where he died the following month.

On his accession to the throne, Louis XVI gave his grandfather's estate to Queen Marie-Antoinette, who retained most of the interior decoration designed by Gabriel and simply replaced a staircase and coffee parlour by a boudoir called the room of "moving mirrors". By means of an ingenious mechanism, these mirrors could be made to cover the windows. Completed in 1787, this boudoir, the work of Mique, is undergoing restoration. At present, only the antechamber, dining-room, billiards room and State Cabinet may be visited. These rooms have been entirely restored and the grey of the wainscoting, a 19th century fashion, has been replaced by its original delicate hues of lime-green and white. As for the furnishings, they were scattered during the Revolution. Those here today closely resemble the originals, particularly because the curtains and silks of the seats were rewoven identically to the 18th century fabrics. The only original pieces of the Small Trianon's furniture which will be able to be returned here on completion of restoration are the famous "pastoral motif" seats, painted in various colours and delivered by Jacob in 1787, and the clock and console-table created at the same time for the Queen's bedchamber.

On taking possession of the Small Trianon, Marie-Antoinette almost immediately had the painter, Hubert Robert, turn the gardens into the English park we see today. A theatre erected in 1780 is hidden in the greenery, its presence revealed only by the porch adorned with a pediment carved by Deschamps. In this theatre, with its interior décor entirely of papier-mâché, the Queen, who loved to act, had Sedaine's comic operas produced and also put on for the first time before the royal family, "the Marriage of Figaro", by Beaumarchais, with the Comte d'Artois, the future Charles X, as Figaro.

The French Pavilion (2)

In the gardens, with an artificial river, Richard Mique, the Queen's architect, erected the Temple of Love in 1778 on a small island and, on the banks of a lake, the Belvedere or Rock Pavilion, in the neo-classical style. Its interior is adorned with delicate arabesques by Richier and a ceiling painted by Lagrenée. Nowadays, the Queen's Garden has undoubtedly won particular renown for the Hamlet which she commissioned Mique to build for her in 1783. Of the twelve houses, based on those in Normandy, which once formed this village, ten still remain. These include, in particular, the Queen's Cottage, linked by a wooden arcade to the Billiards

The Rock Pavilion or Belvedere (4)

The Temple of Love (15)

123

PLAN OF TRIANON

A. *The Entrance Gates*
B. *The Trianon arm of the Canal*
C. *The Grand Trianon*
D. *The Grand Trianon Gardens*

1. *The Small Trianon*
2. *The French Pavilion*
3. *Marie-Antoinette's Theatre*
4. *The Small Lake, the Belvedere and the Grotto*
5. *The Trianon Orangery*
6. *The Great Lake and, on its banks, the Hamlet*
7. *The Fishery and Dairy*
8. *The Ballroom*
9. *The Farm*
10. *The Dovecot*
11. *The Queen's Cottage*
12. *The "Réchauffoir"*
13. *The Boudoir*
14. *The Mill*
15. *The Temple of Love*

The Mill (14) on a summer evening

House, as well as the Mill and the Dairy, next to the Fishery Tower. The latter is also called the "Marlborough Tower" after the song, "Marlborough s'en va-t-en guerre", which the Dauphin's nurse, "Madame Poitrine", had made fashionable. The simple life led by the Queen at Trianon was considered too frivolous by her contemporaries. The festivities and expense, as well as the Queen's entourage of young people known only "for their levity and irresponsibility" aroused general discontent. After the Revolution, the Small Trianon was stripped of its furnishings and rented out for music and dancing. Then, under the Empire, Napoleon gave it first to his sister, Pauline Borghese, and later to his second wife, Empress Marie-Louise.

Louis-Philippe gave it to the Duc and Duchesse d'Orléans, who stayed there often. However, it was Empress Eugénie, a great admirer of Marie-Antoinette, who set out, during the Universal Exhibition of 1867, to refurnish the Small Trianon as it had been in the 18th century. Following the Second Empire nothing further was done until today when an attempt is being made to restore to a more historically authentic state the small estate desired by Louis XV and made famous by Marie-Antoinette.

The Queen's Cottage (11) ▶
in autumn

GENEALOGY OF THE ROYAL FAMILY AT THE TIME OF VERSAILLES

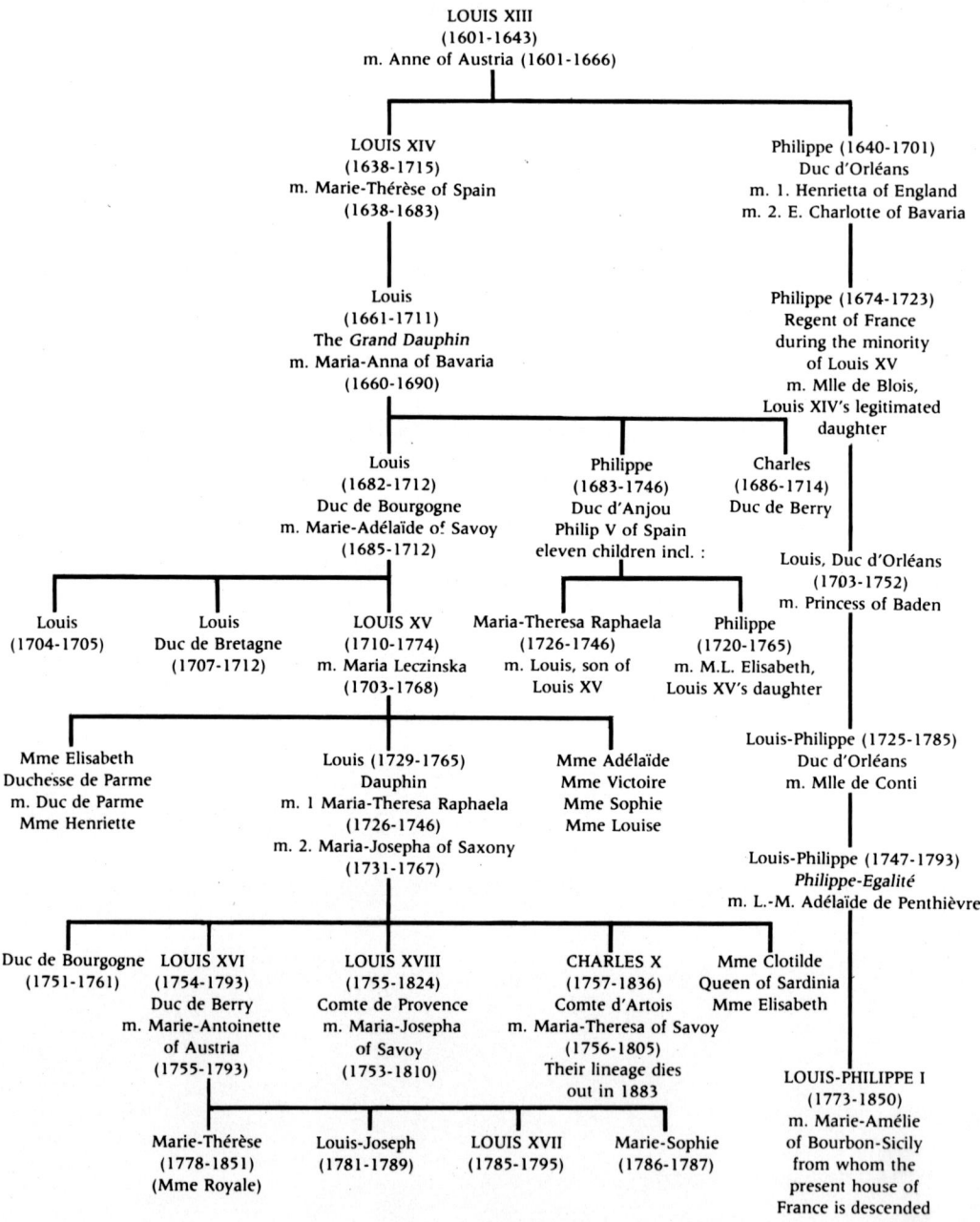